NEW TRADERS' MISTAKES

A Guide to get rid of Common Mistakes

by

Lalit Mohanty

PREFACE

Welcome to "New Traders' Mistakes," a comprehensive guide designed to illuminate the common pitfalls encountered by those venturing into the exciting yet challenging world of trading. In the dynamic landscape of financial markets, navigating the complexities demands a strategic approach and a keen understanding of the nuances involved.

As a new trader, the journey can be both thrilling and perilous. Success in trading requires more than just a willingness to take risks; it demands a nuanced understanding of the markets, a disciplined mindset, and a commitment to learning from both successes and setbacks.

This book is born out of a recognition that every trader embarks on this journey with dreams of financial independence and wealth creation. However, the path to success is riddled with potential missteps, and recognizing these pitfalls early on can make the difference between thriving and merely surviving in the markets.

"New Traders' Mistakes" is not just a compilation of errors; it is a roadmap for avoiding them. Each chapter delves into a specific aspect of trading, dissecting common mistakes and providing insights on how to sidestep them. Whether you're just starting or have a bit of experience under your belt, this book aims to equip you with the knowledge and tools necessary to make informed decisions and cultivate a resilient, long-term approach to trading.

The journey of a trader is one of continual growth and adaptation. Mistakes are inevitable, but the key lies in learning from them, refining your strategies, and honing your skills. With diligence, education, and a commitment to self-improvement, you can transform these mistakes into stepping stones toward your financial goals.

So, as you embark on this educational journey through the pages of "New Traders' Mistakes," consider it not just a guide but a companion in your quest for trading mastery. May the insights within these chapters serve as a beacon, helping you navigate the challenges, avoid the common pitfalls, and emerge as a seasoned and successful trader.

Table of Contents

Chapter 1: The Rush to Riches

- Understanding the importance of patience and realistic expectations.

Chapter 2: Ignoring the Basics

- The significance of a strong foundation in market fundamentals.

Chapter 3: Overlooking Risk Management

- How inadequate risk management can lead to devastating losses.

Chapter 4: Chasing Trends Blindly

- The dangers of following market trends without proper analysis.

Chapter 5: Emotional Trading

- Managing emotions and making decisions based on logic rather than fear or greed.

Chapter 6: Lack of Research

- The value of thorough research before making any trading decisions.

Chapter 7: Neglecting Technical Analysis

- The role of technical analysis in identifying entry and exit points.

Chapter 8: Overtrading

- The pitfalls of excessive trading and its impact on long-term success.

Chapter 9: No Trading Plan

- The importance of a well-defined trading plan for consistent results.

Chapter 10: Falling for Hype

- How to distinguish between genuine opportunities and market hype.

Chapter 11: FOMO (Fear of Missing Out)

- Overcoming the fear of missing out and making rational decisions.

Chapter 12: Poor Record-Keeping

- The necessity of maintaining detailed trading records for analysis.

Chapter 13: Lack of Continuous Learning

- Staying updated with market trends and continuously improving skills.

Chapter 14: Trading without Discipline

- The role of discipline in executing a trading plan consistently.

Chapter 15: Inadequate Capital Management

- Allocating capital wisely to withstand market fluctuations.

Chapter 16: Trading Against the Trend

- The risks associated with going against prevailing market trends.

Chapter 17: Ignoring Market Sentiment

- Incorporating market sentiment analysis for better decision-making.

Chapter 18: Dependence on Tips and Rumors

- Relying on verified information rather than market rumors.

Chapter 19: Impulsive Decision-Making

- Avoiding impulsive decisions that can lead to regrettable outcomes.

Chapter 20: Disregarding Global Events

- Understanding the impact of global events on financial markets.

Chapter 21: Unchecked Leverage

- The dangers of excessive leverage and its potential for huge losses.

Chapter 22: Trading without a Safety Net

- The importance of having an emergency fund for trading uncertainties.

Chapter 23: Neglecting Personal Well-being

- Balancing trading with physical and mental well-being.

Chapter 24: Blindly Trusting Experts

- The importance of critical thinking and independent analysis.

Chapter 25: Staying Resilient

- Developing resilience to navigate the inevitable ups and downs of trading.

CHAPTER 1

THE RUSH TO RICHES

The allure of the financial markets is undeniable. The promise of untold riches and the dream of achieving financial freedom draw countless individuals into the world of trading. However, the journey from novice to seasoned trader is rife with challenges, and one of the earliest and most common mistakes is succumbing to the "Rush to Riches" mentality.

The Illusion of Overnight Success

As new traders set foot into the markets, there is often a palpable eagerness to make substantial profits quickly. The allure of success stories, where individuals seemingly turn a modest investment into a fortune overnight, can be intoxicating. The desire for instant gratification can lead to impulsive decision-making, overlooking critical aspects of trading such as risk management and strategic planning.

Patience as a Virtue

The first lesson every trader must internalize is the virtue of patience. Successful trading is not a sprint; it's a marathon. The financial markets are dynamic and unpredictable, and success is not guaranteed in the short term. Patience is not simply the ability to wait; it's the capacity to maintain composure and discipline during periods of uncertainty.

Setting Realistic Expectations

The rush to riches often stems from unrealistic expectations. It's crucial for new traders to understand that losses are an inherent part of the trading journey. The markets are not a magic wellspring of guaranteed profits; they are a dynamic ecosystem where gains and losses coexist. Realistic expectations set the foundation for a rational and measured approach to trading.

The Perils of Overleveraging

In the pursuit of quick riches, some traders fall prey to the temptation of overleveraging their positions. While leverage can amplify gains, it also magnifies losses. New traders must grasp the delicate balance between risk and reward, avoiding the pitfall of excessive leverage that can lead to a swift erosion of capital.

Cultivating a Long-Term Mindset

Trading is not about quick wins; it's about sustainable success over the long haul. The most prosperous traders understand the importance of continuous learning, adapting to market conditions, and refining their strategies. A long-term mindset fosters resilience, allowing traders to weather the inevitable storms and emerge stronger on the other side.

Conclusion

In the "Rush to Riches," the greatest wealth lies not in hasty gains but in the wisdom gained through experience. This chapter serves as a foundational reminder to new traders: success is a journey, not a destination. Embrace patience, set realistic expectations, and cultivate the mindset required for enduring success in the dynamic world of trading.

As you embark on your trading journey, remember that wealth is not an overnight phenomenon. It is the result of careful planning, disciplined execution, and a commitment to the principles explored in this chapter. May your path be guided by patience and wisdom, laying the groundwork for a prosperous and sustainable trading career.

CHAPTER 2

IGNORING THE BASICS

In the pursuit of trading success, it's easy for new traders to become enamored with complex strategies, intricate technical indicators, and the allure of sophisticated trading platforms. However, the gravest oversight that many make is "Ignoring the Basics." This chapter delves into the fundamental building blocks of successful trading, emphasizing the critical role that a strong foundation in market fundamentals plays in achieving sustainable and informed decision-making.

The Allure of Complexity

In the rapidly evolving world of finance, it's tempting to dive headfirst into advanced trading techniques and intricate market analyses. However, the irony lies in the fact that the most successful traders often attribute their achievements to a deep understanding of the basics. Ignoring these foundational principles can lead to a shaky trading structure, akin to constructing a skyscraper on an unstable foundation.

Market Fundamentals: The Cornerstone

Market fundamentals encompass a broad range of economic indicators, geopolitical events, and macroeconomic trends that influence financial markets. From interest rates and inflation to economic growth and geopolitical stability, these factors create the backdrop against which all trading decisions unfold. Neglecting to grasp these fundamentals is akin to navigating uncharted waters without a compass.

Economic Indicators and Their Impact

New traders must familiarize themselves with key economic indicators such as GDP, unemployment rates, and consumer confidence. These indicators provide invaluable insights into the health of economies, shaping market sentiment and influencing asset prices. Ignoring these signals is akin to flying blind, leaving traders vulnerable to unforeseen turbulence in the markets.

Technical Analysis Alone Is Not Enough

While technical analysis is a powerful tool, relying solely on charts and indicators without understanding the underlying fundamentals is a recipe for disaster. The most successful traders seamlessly integrate both technical and fundamental analyses, recognizing that these approaches provide a comprehensive view of market dynamics.

Risk and Reward: A Fundamental Equation

Understanding risk and reward is fundamental to successful trading. Ignoring this basic equation can lead to reckless decision-making, with potential consequences ranging from minor setbacks to catastrophic losses. Establishing a risk management strategy based on solid fundamentals is the bedrock of a resilient trading approach.

Continuous Learning and Adaptation

Markets are dynamic, and the fundamentals that drive them can shift rapidly. Ignoring the basics means neglecting the need for continuous learning and adaptation. Successful traders stay abreast of economic developments, policy changes, and global events, adjusting their strategies to align with the ever-changing market landscape.

Conclusion

"Ignoring the Basics" is a pitfall that new traders cannot afford to stumble into. This chapter serves as a clarion call to prioritize the development of a strong foundation in market fundamentals. As you navigate the complex and dynamic world of trading, remember that success is built on a bedrock of understanding the basics—economic indicators, market trends, and the delicate balance of risk and reward.

Embrace the fundamentals, for they are the compass guiding you through the labyrinth of financial markets. May your trading journey be anchored in a robust understanding of the basics, paving the way for informed decisions and long-term success.

CHAPTER 3

OVERLOOKING RISK MANAGEMENT

In the high-stakes arena of trading, where fortunes can be made or lost in the blink of an eye, one of the gravest mistakes a new trader can make is "Overlooking Risk Management." This chapter delves into the critical importance of implementing sound risk management practices and explores the dire consequences that can unfold when this fundamental aspect of trading is neglected.

The Illusion of Invincibility

New traders often enter the markets fueled by enthusiasm and a sense of invincibility. The focus tends to be on potential profits, overshadowing the equally vital consideration of potential losses. Overlooking risk management is akin to setting sail without a compass—traders may be moving, but the direction is uncertain, and the dangers are amplified.

The Role of Risk Management

At its core, risk management is the compass that guides traders through the unpredictable waters of the financial markets. It involves assessing potential risks, defining acceptable levels of exposure, and implementing strategies to mitigate the impact of adverse market movements. Neglecting these crucial steps can expose traders to catastrophic financial storms.

The 2% Rule and Position Sizing

One fundamental principle of risk management is the 2% rule, which advises that no single trade should risk more than 2% of the trader's total capital. Additionally, thoughtful position sizing ensures that the impact of a losing trade is limited, preventing a single setback from eroding a substantial portion of the trading capital. Ignoring these principles is a recipe for financial disaster.

Emotional Impact of Unchecked Risk

Inadequate risk management not only jeopardizes financial well-being but also takes a toll on the trader's emotional state. Large losses can trigger panic, fear, and irrational decision-making, leading to a vicious cycle of compounding losses. Overlooking risk management sets the stage for a destructive emotional rollercoaster that can derail even the most promising trading careers.

Diversification as a Risk Mitigation Strategy

A well-rounded risk management strategy incorporates diversification—spreading investments across different assets or markets to reduce overall risk. Ignoring the importance of a diversified portfolio leaves traders vulnerable to the impact of a single adverse event or market downturn.

Continuous Monitoring and Adjustment

Risk management is not a one-time task; it's an ongoing process that requires constant monitoring and adjustment. Markets evolve, and risks change. Failing to adapt to these shifts can render initially effective risk management strategies obsolete.

Conclusion

"Overlooking Risk Management" is a perilous oversight that no trader can afford. This chapter serves as a stark reminder of the consequences that can unfold when risk is not adequately managed. As you navigate the intricate world of trading, remember that preserving capital is as crucial as generating profits.

Implementing sound risk management practices is not a sign of weakness but a testament to prudence and foresight. May your trading journey be marked by the wisdom to manage risk effectively, ensuring that the storms of market volatility strengthen rather than shatter your path to long-term success.

CHAPTER 4

CHASING TRENDS BLINDLY

In the ever-shifting landscape of financial markets, the allure of market trends can be intoxicating. Yet, one of the most prevalent mistakes made by new traders is "Chasing Trends Blindly." This chapter unravels the dangers of impulsively following market trends without the requisite analysis, shedding light on the potential pitfalls that await those who succumb to the temptation of trend-chasing.

The Seductive Allure of Trends

Market trends, whether bullish or bearish, exert a magnetic pull on traders seeking quick and substantial gains. The idea of riding the wave of a trend to profitability can be enticing, fostering a mentality of 'the trend is your friend.' However, blindly embracing this notion without proper scrutiny can lead to financial shipwrecks.

The Importance of Analysis

Chasing trends blindly implies an absence of thorough analysis—a critical misstep in the trader's journey. Proper analysis involves evaluating the fundamentals, considering technical indicators, and understanding market sentiment.

Neglecting these elements leaves traders susceptible to the whims of market fluctuations and sudden reversals.

The Risk of Late Entry

New traders often fall into the trap of chasing a trend after it has already gained significant momentum. This "late entry" risk exposes traders to the danger of buying at the peak or selling at the bottom, eroding potential profits and amplifying losses. The mantra of 'buy low, sell high' becomes an elusive pursuit when trends are chased without prudence.

The Mirage of Perpetual Trends

Markets, by nature, are cyclical and subject to reversals. Chasing trends blindly assumes that current market conditions will persist indefinitely. The reality, however, is that trends exhaust themselves, giving way to corrections and reversals. Traders who fail to recognize this inevitability may find themselves on the wrong side of a sudden and adverse market shift.

Overlooking Contrarian Opportunities

Blindly following trends can lead traders to overlook valuable contrarian opportunities. Contrarian strategies involve going against prevailing market sentiment, and while they carry their own risks, they also present the potential for substantial gains when timed correctly. Ignoring contrarian perspectives limits a trader's toolkit and exposes them to unnecessary risks.

The Need for a Balanced Approach

The key lies in striking a balance between acknowledging and leveraging trends and maintaining a critical perspective.

Successful traders combine trend analysis with a nuanced understanding of market dynamics, allowing them to make informed decisions rather than succumbing to impulsive actions driven solely by prevailing trends.

Conclusion

"Chasing Trends Blindly" is a pitfall that can undermine the aspirations of even the most promising traders. This chapter serves as a cautionary tale, urging traders to approach trends with a discerning eye. In the quest for profitability, remember that successful trading involves not only recognizing trends but also understanding when to embrace, challenge, or step aside from them.

CHAPTER 5

EMOTIONAL TRADING

The world of trading is a psychological battlefield, where emotions can be both a trader's greatest asset and their most formidable adversary. "Emotional Trading" explores the impact of unchecked feelings on decision-making, shedding light on the dangers of succumbing to fear, greed, and other emotional pitfalls that can derail even the most well-thought-out trading strategies.

The Emotional Rollercoaster

Trading is inherently emotional. The adrenaline rush of a successful trade and the sting of a loss can trigger powerful emotions. However, allowing emotions to dictate trading decisions can lead to impulsive actions, clouded judgment, and ultimately, financial distress.

Fear and Paralysis

Fear is a natural response to uncertainty, and in the world of trading, uncertainty is a constant companion. Traders plagued by fear may hesitate to execute trades, miss profitable opportunities, or exit positions prematurely. Overcoming the paralyzing grip of fear is essential for executing a well-defined trading plan.

Greed and Overtrading

Conversely, greed can drive traders to overreach and overtrade. The insatiable desire for more profits can lead to excessive risk-taking, disregarding established strategies, and entering trades impulsively. Recognizing and curbing the influence of greed is vital for maintaining discipline and preserving capital.

Impatience and the Urge for Instant Gratification

In the fast-paced world of trading, impatience is a common emotional hurdle. The desire for instant gratification can lead to rash decision-making, overlooking crucial analysis, and succumbing to the allure of short-term gains. Patience, a cornerstone of successful trading, becomes elusive in the face of unchecked impatience.

Regret and Hindsight Bias

After a trade concludes, it's easy to fall into the trap of regret and hindsight bias. Traders may second-guess their decisions, convinced they could have predicted market movements with perfect foresight. Managing regret involves learning from experiences without dwelling on past missteps, recognizing that the markets are inherently uncertain.

Developing Emotional Intelligence

Successful traders cultivate emotional intelligence—a heightened awareness of their emotions and the ability to manage them effectively. This involves recognizing emotional triggers, implementing coping mechanisms, and making decisions based on logic rather than impulsive reactions.

Tools for Emotional Discipline

Implementing tools such as trading journals, mindfulness practices, and pre-established rules can provide a structured framework for emotional discipline. Regular reflection on past trades and emotional states can foster self-awareness, empowering traders to make more rational decisions in the heat of the moment.

Conclusion

"Emotional Trading" is a formidable adversary that every trader must face. This chapter underscores the importance of developing emotional intelligence as a critical component of successful trading. As you navigate the emotional rollercoaster of the markets, remember that discipline, self-awareness, and a commitment to logical decision-making are your greatest allies.

.

CHAPTER 6

LACK OF RESEARCH

In the fast-paced world of trading, where markets can shift in the blink of an eye, the value of thorough research cannot be overstated. "Lack of Research" is a pitfall that ensnares many new traders, luring them into impulsive decisions driven by incomplete information. This chapter explores the critical importance of diligent research before making any trading decisions.

The Temptation of Quick Decisions

The urgency of market movements can tempt traders to skip the vital step of research and dive headfirst into trades. The allure of quick profits may overshadow the need for a comprehensive understanding of the assets, market conditions, and potential risks. However, what appears as a shortcut to success often leads to unforeseen pitfalls.

The Foundation of Informed Decision-Making

Thorough research forms the bedrock of informed decision-making in the world of trading. It involves a multifaceted approach, encompassing both fundamental and technical analysis. Neglecting this foundational step is akin to setting sail without navigation—a directionless journey fraught with peril.

Fundamental Analysis: Understanding the Underlying Factors

Fundamental analysis involves evaluating the intrinsic value of an asset by examining economic, financial, and qualitative factors. This includes scrutinizing financial statements, assessing economic indicators, and staying abreast of relevant news and events. Lack of research in fundamental analysis leaves traders uninformed about the underlying forces driving asset prices.

Technical Analysis: Deciphering Market Patterns

Technical analysis involves studying historical price charts, patterns, and trading volumes to forecast future price movements. It provides crucial insights into entry and exit points. Disregarding technical analysis means missing out on valuable tools for gauging market sentiment and identifying potential trends and reversals.

Risk Assessment and Management

Research extends beyond asset analysis; it includes evaluating risk factors. Understanding the potential risks associated with a trade is essential for effective risk management. Lack of research in risk assessment can expose traders to unforeseen challenges and jeopardize their capital.

Market Sentiment: The X-Factor

Research also involves gauging market sentiment—understanding how traders feel about an asset or the overall market. Ignoring sentiment analysis means overlooking a significant aspect of market dynamics, potentially leading to misguided decisions based on incomplete information.

Continuous Learning and Adaptation

Markets are dynamic, and research is an ongoing process. Traders who fail to prioritize continuous learning and adaptation risk falling behind. Staying informed about industry trends, global events, and changes in market conditions is crucial for maintaining a competitive edge.

Conclusion

"Lack of Research" is a treacherous path that can undermine even the most promising trading endeavors. This chapter serves as a clarion call for the indispensable role of research in the trader's toolkit. As you navigate the complexities of the financial markets, let this be a reminder that success is cultivated through knowledge, diligence, and a commitment to understanding the intricacies that drive market movements.

CHAPTER 7

NEGLECTING TECHNICAL ANALYSIS

In the intricate tapestry of trading, neglecting the role of technical analysis is a common misstep that can leave traders navigating the markets with only half the toolkit. "Neglecting Technical Analysis" is a pitfall that arises when the significance of charts, patterns, and historical price data is underestimated. This chapter explores the vital role of technical analysis in identifying entry and exit points, enhancing decision-making, and contributing to a comprehensive trading strategy.

The Blind Spot in Market Understanding

Technical analysis involves the study of historical market data, primarily price and volume, to forecast future price movements. Neglecting this critical aspect creates a blind spot in a trader's understanding, limiting their ability to interpret market dynamics accurately.

Charts as a Visual Guide

Charts are the visual representation of market movements over time. They offer insights into price trends, support and resistance levels, and potential turning points. Disregarding charts means missing out on a valuable visual guide that can aid in decision-making.

Patterns and Trends: The Language of Markets

Technical analysis allows traders to identify patterns and trends that signify potential market directions. Chart patterns, such as head and shoulders or double tops and bottoms, can provide valuable clues about market sentiment. Neglecting these patterns is akin to trying to understand a foreign language without studying its grammar and syntax.

Support and Resistance: Building Strong Foundations

Support and resistance levels are critical concepts in technical analysis. They represent price levels at which an asset has historically had a difficult time moving above (resistance) or below (support). Neglecting to identify these levels leaves traders without a compass, making it challenging to navigate potential price reversals.

Indicators and Oscillators: Tools of Analysis

Technical indicators and oscillators, ranging from moving averages to the Relative Strength Index (RSI), offer quantifiable measures of market conditions. Ignoring these tools deprives traders of objective metrics that can validate or challenge their assumptions about market trends and potential reversals.

Entry and Exit Points: Precision in Action

One of the primary advantages of technical analysis is its ability to pinpoint entry and exit points. Neglecting this precision means relying on guesswork rather than data-driven decisions. The consequences can range from missed profit opportunities to significant losses.

Risk Management and Technical Analysis

Technical analysis is intertwined with effective risk management. By identifying potential price levels and trends, traders can establish stop-loss orders and manage their risk more effectively. Neglecting this aspect leaves traders vulnerable to unanticipated market movements.

Continuous Learning and Adaptation

Like any facet of trading, technical analysis is not static. Markets evolve, and the effectiveness of technical indicators may change. Traders who neglect the ongoing process of learning and adapting their technical analysis strategies may find themselves ill-prepared for shifting market conditions.

Conclusion

In the journey through the financial markets, neglecting technical analysis is akin to navigating uncharted waters without a reliable map. This chapter emphasizes the importance of embracing the tools and insights that technical analysis provides. As you refine your trading approach, let this be a reminder that success often lies in the details—charts, patterns, and indicators that, when properly understood, empower you to make more informed and strategic decisions.

CHAPTER 8

OVERTRADING

In the pursuit of success in the fast-paced realm of trading, the pitfall of "Overtrading" lurks as a silent adversary, ready to undermine even the most disciplined strategies. This chapter delves into the dangers of excessive trading, exploring how the allure of constant activity can erode capital, hinder performance, and jeopardize the long-term success of traders.

The Allure of Constant Action

The allure of trading is inherently linked to the excitement of making decisions and witnessing market movements in real-time. However, this desire for constant action can spiral into a destructive pattern of overtrading, where the quantity of trades takes precedence over their quality.

The Illusion of Productivity

Overtraders often fall prey to the illusion that constant activity equates to productivity. However, the truth is that more trades do not necessarily translate to more profits. In fact, the constant buying and selling of assets can lead to higher transaction costs, eating into potential gains and amplifying losses.

Quality Over Quantity

Successful trading is about making well-informed, strategic decisions rather than an abundance of impulsive trades. Overtrading dilutes the impact of each decision, making it challenging to focus on thorough analysis, risk management, and the execution of a well-defined trading plan.

Emotional and Psychological Toll

Excessive trading can take a toll on traders emotionally and psychologically. Constantly monitoring the markets and executing trades can lead to burnout, anxiety, and a heightened emotional rollercoaster. Emotional fatigue compromises decision-making, paving the way for impulsive actions.

The Mirage of Short-Term Gains

Overtraders often chase short-term gains without considering the long-term consequences. The focus on immediate profits can lead to a lack of strategic vision, hindering the cultivation of a sustainable and resilient trading approach.

Transaction Costs and Fees

Every trade incurs transaction costs and fees, which can accumulate rapidly with frequent trading. Overtraders may find themselves with significantly diminished profits or even losses after factoring in these expenses.

Straining Risk Management

Effective risk management is contingent on careful consideration of each trade. Overtrading places immense strain on risk management strategies, as the sheer volume of transactions can make it challenging to monitor and control potential risks.

The Importance of Patience

Patience is a virtue in trading, and successful traders understand the value of waiting for optimal setups. Overtrading is antithetical to patience, fostering a mindset of constant urgency that can lead to poor decision-making and missed opportunities for high-probability trades.

Conclusion

"Overtrading" is a pitfall that can undermine the foundation of a trader's success. This chapter serves as a reminder that quality triumphs over quantity in the world of trading. As you navigate the complexities of financial markets, resist the allure of overtrading, and let patience, discipline, and strategic decision-making guide your journey.

CHAPTER 9

NO TRADING PLAN

In the chaotic arena of trading, navigating without a clear roadmap can lead to perilous consequences. "No Trading Plan" is a common misstep that new traders make, often underestimating the profound impact a well-defined plan can have on their success. This chapter delves into the critical importance of having a structured trading plan for achieving consistent results and weathering the unpredictable nature of financial markets.

The Void of Direction

Trading without a plan is akin to setting sail without a destination. It leaves traders adrift in the vast sea of market volatility, vulnerable to impulsive decisions, emotional reactions, and the whims of market trends.

The Blueprint for Success

A trading plan is the blueprint that outlines a trader's approach to the markets. It encompasses key elements such as trading goals, risk tolerance, entry and exit criteria, and strategies for managing both profits and losses. Neglecting this foundational document is like embarking on a construction project without architectural drawings—a recipe for instability and failure.

Defining Clear Objectives

A well-crafted trading plan starts with clear and realistic objectives. Whether the goal is capital preservation, steady income, or long-term growth, having a defined purpose provides direction and clarity, guiding every decision made in the markets.

Risk Management: The Guardian of Capital

A trading plan lays out specific risk management strategies, including the acceptable level of risk per trade, stop-loss orders, and position sizing. Trading without a plan neglects these safeguards, exposing traders to unnecessary risks that can have catastrophic consequences on their capital.

Entry and Exit Criteria

Successful trades are not just about picking the right assets; they are about entering and exiting at the right times. A trading plan outlines specific criteria for entering a trade, as well as conditions for closing positions. Absence of a plan leaves traders vulnerable to impulsive decisions driven by emotions rather than logic.

Consistency in Decision-Making

Consistency is a hallmark of successful traders. A trading plan provides a structured framework that promotes consistency in decision-making. Without a plan, decisions become arbitrary, and the lack of consistency can lead to erratic performance.

Adapting to Market Conditions

While a trading plan provides structure, it should also be flexible enough to adapt to changing market conditions. Trading without a plan makes it challenging to navigate evolving landscapes, leaving traders ill-prepared for shifts in volatility, trends, or economic factors.

Psychological Support

A trading plan serves as psychological support during times of uncertainty. It provides a reference point for traders to anchor their decisions, mitigating the impact of emotional reactions to market fluctuations.

Conclusion

"No Trading Plan" is a perilous void that can undermine the very essence of trading success. This chapter emphasizes the indispensable role of a well-defined plan in the trader's arsenal. As you venture into the unpredictable terrain of financial markets, let this be a reminder that success is not accidental—it's a result of deliberate planning, disciplined execution, and a commitment to the principles outlined in a comprehensive trading plan.

CHAPTER 10

FALLING FOR HYPE

In the ever-evolving landscape of financial markets, the siren call of hype can be irresistible. "Falling for Hype" is a common pitfall that ensnares traders, leading them to make impulsive decisions driven by exaggerated promises, sensational news, or the allure of quick riches. This chapter explores the dangers of succumbing to market hype and provides insights on how to distinguish between genuine opportunities and fleeting fads.

The Allure of Exaggeration

Market hype is like a captivating melody that lures traders with promises of astronomical returns, revolutionary technologies, or unprecedented opportunities. Falling for hype can be seductive, clouding judgment and leading traders down a path of impulsive decisions.

Distinguishing Genuine Opportunities

Distinguishing between genuine opportunities and market hype requires a discerning eye. Genuine opportunities are grounded in sound fundamentals, supported by thorough research, and aligned with a trader's risk tolerance and financial goals. Hype, on the other hand, often lacks substance and is fueled by sensationalism.

Thorough Due Diligence

Before succumbing to the allure of a hyped-up asset or market trend, conduct thorough due diligence. Research the fundamentals, assess the credibility of information sources, and critically evaluate the long-term viability of the opportunity. Hype tends to fade when exposed to the scrutiny of meticulous investigation.

Historical Context and Patterns

Examine historical patterns and contextualize current hype within the broader market trends. Genuine opportunities often have a foundation in long-term market dynamics, while hype tends to be short-lived and lacks sustained upward momentum.

Risk-Reward Analysis

Consider the risk-reward ratio of the hyped opportunity. Assess the potential downsides as rigorously as the promised upsides. Genuine opportunities offer a balanced risk-reward profile, while hype often involves a disproportionate level of risk.

Emotional Detachment

Maintain emotional detachment when evaluating market opportunities. Hype can trigger emotional responses such as fear of missing out (FOMO) or irrational exuberance. A disciplined and rational approach helps in distinguishing genuine opportunities from emotionally charged hype.

Avoiding Herd Mentality

Hype often spreads through a herd mentality, where traders follow the crowd without independent analysis. Resist the urge to join the herd and make decisions based on your own research, analysis, and trading plan.

Seeking Diverse Perspectives

Engage with a variety of perspectives and seek insights from experienced traders, analysts, and industry experts. Genuine opportunities withstand scrutiny, and diverse perspectives can provide a more comprehensive view, helping you make informed decisions.

Continuous Learning and Adaptation

Market dynamics evolve, and what may seem like hype today might transform into a genuine opportunity tomorrow. Stay vigilant, continuously learn, and adapt your trading strategies based on evolving market conditions.

CHAPTER 11

FOMO (FEAR OF MISSING OUT)

In the fast-paced realm of trading, the specter of FOMO (Fear of Missing Out) looms large. This psychological phenomenon can drive traders to make impulsive decisions, chase trends, and abandon rational strategies in pursuit of perceived opportunities. This chapter explores the dangers of FOMO and provides insights on how to overcome this powerful emotion, ensuring that decisions are driven by logic rather than the fear of missing out.

The Allure of Immediate Gratification

FOMO is fueled by the desire for immediate gratification, the fear that others are profiting while one is left on the sidelines. This urgency can lead to hasty decisions, impulsive trades, and a departure from a well-defined trading plan.

Recognizing FOMO Triggers

Understanding FOMO begins with recognizing its triggers. Whether it's the hype surrounding a hot asset, the fear of missing a trend, or the pressure to conform to market sentiment, being aware of these triggers is the first step in overcoming the fear of missing out.

Anchoring Decisions in Analysis

To overcome FOMO, anchor your decisions in thorough analysis and a well-defined trading plan. Base your actions on a comprehensive understanding of market fundamentals, technical indicators, and risk-reward considerations rather than succumbing to the emotional pull of missing out on potential gains.

Embracing a Patient Mindset

Patience is the antidote to FOMO. Recognize that markets are dynamic, opportunities are abundant, and there will always be another trade. A patient mindset allows you to wait for optimal setups and make decisions based on careful consideration rather than the fear of missing out.

Setting Realistic Expectations

FOMO often arises from unrealistic expectations of quick and substantial gains. Set realistic expectations for your trading journey. Understand that success takes time, and avoiding the fear of missing out means embracing a long-term perspective focused on sustainable growth.

Learning from Missed Opportunities

Rather than viewing missed opportunities as losses, see them as learning experiences. Analyze the reasons behind the missed trade, assess whether it aligns with your trading strategy, and use the insights gained to refine your approach. Every missed opportunity is a chance to enhance your skills.

Utilizing Limit Orders

To counteract impulsive actions driven by FOMO, use limit orders. Set predefined entry and exit points based on your analysis and trading plan. This approach not only mitigates the influence of emotions but also ensures that your trades align with your predetermined strategy.

Building Emotional Resilience

Overcoming FOMO requires emotional resilience. Cultivate self-awareness, recognize when emotions are influencing your decisions, and develop coping mechanisms to stay focused and disciplined during periods of market excitement.

Continuous Reflection and Improvement

Regularly reflect on your trading decisions and outcomes. Understand the role that FOMO played in past actions, and strive for continuous improvement. The ability to learn from experiences and adapt your approach is essential for overcoming the fear of missing out.

Conclusion

"FOMO (Fear of Missing Out)" is a psychological challenge that every trader encounters. This chapter emphasizes the importance of mastering this emotion to make rational decisions in the dynamic world of trading. As you navigate the markets, let this be a reminder that success is not measured by the trades you take in haste but by the disciplined and calculated decisions that lead to long-term prosperity.

CHAPTER 12

POOR RECORD-KEEPING

In the intricate tapestry of trading, the significance of meticulous record-keeping often goes underestimated. "Poor Record-Keeping" is a pitfall that can hinder a trader's ability to learn, adapt, and make informed decisions. This chapter explores the necessity of maintaining detailed trading records, emphasizing how thorough documentation is not only a regulatory requirement but a vital tool for personal growth and long-term success in the financial markets.

The Forgotten Trail

Poor record-keeping is akin to embarking on a journey without a map or compass. It leaves traders navigating the complexities of the markets without a clear trail of their past decisions, successes, and mistakes. Without this historical context, traders risk repeating errors and missing opportunities for improvement.

The Blueprint for Improvement

Detailed trading records serve as a blueprint for improvement. They provide a comprehensive view of your trading history, enabling you to identify patterns, assess the effectiveness of your strategies, and make informed adjustments. Without this roadmap, the path to improvement becomes a convoluted maze.

Learning from Mistakes

Mistakes are an inevitable part of trading. However, their value lies in the lessons they impart. Without accurate records, it's challenging to pinpoint where and why mistakes occurred. Detailed records serve as a repository of valuable insights, allowing you to learn from missteps and refine your approach.

Analyzing Successes

Just as important as learning from mistakes is analyzing successful trades. Detailed records enable you to deconstruct winning strategies, identify the factors that contributed to success, and replicate effective approaches in future trades. Without this analysis, replicating success becomes a game of chance rather than strategy.

Regulatory Compliance

Beyond personal development, maintaining detailed trading records is often a regulatory requirement. Adhering to these regulations ensures transparency, accountability, and compliance with financial authorities. Poor record-keeping not only jeopardizes your trading success but may also lead to legal and regulatory consequences.

Building Discipline

Recording every trade forces discipline into your trading routine. It instills a habit of precision, making you more conscious of your decisions and the importance of following your trading plan. Poor record-keeping, on the other hand, fosters a lax approach, eroding the foundations of disciplined trading.

The Anatomy of a Trading Journal

A trading journal is a trader's most potent tool for record-keeping. It typically includes details such as entry and exit points, trade size, risk-reward ratios, market conditions, and emotional states during trades. The comprehensive information captured in a trading journal is invaluable for self-assessment and continuous improvement.

Tools for Record-Keeping

In the digital age, numerous tools and platforms facilitate effective record-keeping. From dedicated trading journal apps to spreadsheet software, find a method that suits your preferences and ensures that every trade is documented accurately and comprehensively.

Continuous Adaptation

Markets evolve, strategies need refinement, and traders must adapt to changing conditions. Detailed records provide the foundation for this adaptation. Regularly revisiting your trading journal and analyzing past performance allows you to stay ahead of market trends, refine your strategies, and remain competitive.

Conclusion

"Poor Record-Keeping" is a perilous oversight that can impede the progress of even the most seasoned traders. This chapter underscores the indispensable role of detailed record-keeping in the trader's toolkit. As you navigate the ever-changing currents of financial markets, let this be a reminder that success is not just about making trades; it's about understanding, adapting, and learning from every facet of your trading journey.

CHAPTER 13

LACK OF CONTINUOUS LEARNING

In the dynamic and ever-evolving world of trading, stagnation is a silent adversary that can erode the foundations of success. "Lack of Continuous Learning" is a pitfall that ensnares traders who fail to adapt, stay informed, and continuously refine their skills. This chapter explores the critical importance of staying updated with market trends and the ongoing pursuit of knowledge to ensure a trader's longevity and prosperity in the financial markets.

The Perils of Stagnation

Markets are in a constant state of flux, influenced by economic shifts, geopolitical events, and technological advancements. Traders who fail to embrace continuous learning risk falling behind, becoming obsolete in the face of evolving market dynamics.

Embracing a Growth Mindset

Continuous learning is not just about acquiring new information; it's a mindset—a commitment to growth and adaptation. Traders with a growth mindset view challenges as opportunities to learn, mistakes as stepping stones to improvement, and success as a journey rather than a destination.

Staying Informed with Market Trends

Market trends are not static; they ebb and flow in response to a myriad of factors. Traders who remain stagnant miss out on the valuable insights that come from understanding and adapting to shifting market conditions. Continuous learning ensures that you stay ahead of trends and make informed decisions.

Adapting to Technological Changes

The financial industry is continually transformed by technological advancements. From algorithmic trading to blockchain technology, staying abreast of these changes is essential for making informed decisions and leveraging new tools that can enhance trading strategies.

The Role of Education

Formal and informal education play crucial roles in a trader's journey. Whether through books, online courses, webinars, or mentorship programs, actively seeking education allows traders to deepen their understanding of market principles, technical analysis, and trading strategies.

Learning from Industry Experts

Engaging with and learning from industry experts can provide invaluable insights. Whether through conferences, forums, or networking events, the opportunity to exchange ideas with experienced traders fosters a rich learning environment and exposes traders to diverse perspectives.

Reflecting on Past Trades

Continuous learning involves reflecting on past trades. Analyze both successes and failures, identifying patterns and lessons that can inform future decisions. This introspective process is a key element of refining strategies and improving overall trading performance.

Experimentation and Innovation

Traders who embrace continuous learning are more open to experimentation and innovation. Trying new strategies, exploring different asset classes, and adapting to emerging trends are hallmarks of traders committed to evolving with the market.

Fostering a Community of Learners

Joining or forming a community of like-minded learners can amplify the benefits of continuous learning. The exchange of ideas, shared experiences, and collective knowledge create a supportive ecosystem that propels individual and collective growth.

Conclusion

"Lack of Continuous Learning" is a pitfall that can consign traders to the sidelines in an industry that thrives on innovation and adaptation. This chapter emphasizes the perpetual importance of staying informed, adapting to change, and fostering a commitment to continuous improvement. As you navigate the complexities of financial markets, let this be a reminder that success is not a static destination; it's a dynamic journey marked by a dedication to lifelong learning and the relentless pursuit of excellence.

CHAPTER 14

TRADING WITHOUT DISCIPLINE

Discipline is the backbone of successful trading, a guiding force that ensures traders adhere to their plans even in the face of market uncertainties and emotional challenges. "Trading without Discipline" is a perilous pitfall that can unravel even the most promising strategies, leading to impulsive decisions, erratic behavior, and ultimately, poor outcomes. This chapter explores the indispensable role of discipline in executing a trading plan consistently and safeguarding long-term success in the financial markets.

The Erosion of Discipline

Discipline is the bedrock upon which a trader's success is built. It involves the consistent execution of a well-defined trading plan, adherence to risk management strategies, and the resilience to withstand the emotional rollercoaster of market fluctuations. Trading without discipline erodes this foundation, exposing traders to unnecessary risks and compromising their ability to make rational decisions.

The Importance of a Trading Plan

A trading plan is only as effective as its execution. Discipline ensures that every element of the plan, from entry and exit points to risk management strategies, is followed meticulously. Trading without discipline transforms a robust plan into a mere set of guidelines, susceptible to the whims of emotions and market pressures.

Emotional Resilience

Discipline is a shield against emotional turmoil. Traders who lack discipline are vulnerable to the whims of fear and greed, leading to impulsive decisions and erratic behavior. Emotional resilience, cultivated through disciplined execution, allows traders to navigate market fluctuations with composure and focus.

Consistency in Decision-Making

Successful traders are characterized by consistency in decision-making. Discipline ensures that each trade is executed with the same level of precision and adherence to the established plan. Trading without discipline introduces variability, making it challenging to evaluate the effectiveness of strategies and identify areas for improvement.

Risk Management as a Pillar of Discipline

Effective risk management is an integral part of disciplined trading. It involves setting predetermined risk levels, utilizing stop-loss orders, and sizing positions appropriately. Trading without discipline in risk management exposes traders to excessive risks and jeopardizes capital preservation.

Avoiding Impulsive Actions

Impulsive actions are the nemesis of disciplined trading. Whether triggered by market fluctuations, external news, or emotional responses, impulsive decisions can lead to significant losses. Discipline serves as a deterrent to impulsive actions, fostering a methodical and rational approach to decision-making.

Developing Routine and Structure

Discipline thrives in routine and structure. Traders who adhere to a consistent trading routine are better equipped to maintain discipline. A structured approach involves pre-market preparations, adherence to trading hours, and a systematic review of trades, fostering a disciplined mindset.

Learning from Mistakes with Discipline

Disciplined traders view mistakes as opportunities for improvement rather than setbacks. When errors occur, discipline enables traders to objectively assess what went wrong, learn from the experience, and make adjustments to prevent recurring mistakes.

Accountability and Responsibility

Discipline instills a sense of accountability and responsibility. Traders who operate with discipline take ownership of their decisions and outcomes. In contrast, trading without discipline may lead to a lack of accountability, with traders blaming external factors for poor performance.

Conclusion

"Trading without Discipline" is a precarious tightrope that jeopardizes the stability of a trader's journey. This chapter underscores the pivotal role of discipline in executing a trading plan consistently. As you navigate the challenges and opportunities of financial markets, let this be a steadfast reminder that success is not just about what you trade but how you trade—marked by unwavering discipline, meticulous execution, and a commitment to the principles that guide your path.

CHAPTER 15

INADEQUATE CAPITAL MANAGEMENT

In the intricate dance of financial markets, the allocation and management of capital are paramount. "Inadequate Capital Management" is a perilous pitfall that can undermine even the most robust trading strategies. This chapter explores the critical importance of allocating capital wisely, safeguarding against risks, and ensuring resilience in the face of market fluctuations.

The Foundation of Long-Term Success

Capital management is the bedrock upon which trading success is built. It involves judiciously allocating funds, setting appropriate position sizes, and implementing strategies to preserve and grow capital. Inadequate capital management places traders on shaky ground, susceptible to the whims of market volatility and unforeseen challenges.

Position Sizing and Risk-Reward Ratios

A cornerstone of capital management is position sizing—determining the amount of capital to allocate to each trade. Inadequate capital management neglects the importance of this crucial step, exposing traders to excessive risks or limiting potential gains. Aligning position sizes with risk-reward ratios is a disciplined approach that ensures capital is deployed strategically.

Preserving Capital in Drawdowns

Markets are unpredictable, and drawdowns are an inevitable part of trading. Inadequate capital management exacerbates the impact of drawdowns, potentially leading to catastrophic losses. Effective capital management ensures that losses are controlled, preserving capital to capitalize on future opportunities.

Diversification as a Risk Mitigation Tool

Diversifying capital across different assets or trading strategies is a risk mitigation tool often overlooked in inadequate capital management. Concentrating capital in a single position or asset class exposes traders to heightened risks. Diversification spreads risk and helps protect capital during periods of market uncertainty.

Adapting to Changing Market Conditions

Capital management is not static; it requires adaptation to changing market conditions. Inadequate capital management lacks the flexibility to adjust position sizes, risk parameters, and overall strategy in response to evolving market dynamics.

Traders who neglect this adaptability risk being ill-prepared for shifts in volatility, trends, or economic factors.

Setting Realistic Expectations

A crucial aspect of capital management is setting realistic expectations for returns. Inadequate capital management often arises from unrealistic profit expectations, leading to aggressive trading strategies that increase the likelihood of significant losses. Realistic expectations ensure a balanced approach to risk and reward.

Utilizing Stop-Loss Orders

Stop-loss orders are a vital tool in capital management. They help limit losses by automatically triggering the sale of an asset when it reaches a predetermined price. Inadequate capital management may involve a lack of discipline in setting and adhering to stop-loss levels, exposing traders to unnecessary risks.

Consistent Evaluation of Capital Allocation

Successful capital management requires ongoing evaluation. Inadequate capital management neglects this aspect, leading to a lack of awareness about the effectiveness of allocation strategies. Regularly assessing capital allocation ensures that traders remain proactive in adapting to market conditions and optimizing their portfolios.

Embracing a Long-Term Perspective

Inadequate capital management often results from a short-term focus on immediate gains. Successful traders recognize the importance of a long-term perspective, where capital is managed with an eye on sustained growth and resilience over time.

Conclusion

"Inadequate Capital Management" is a precipice that traders must navigate with care. This chapter emphasizes the pivotal role of effective capital management in building a resilient and successful trading foundation. As you navigate the dynamic terrain of financial markets, let this serve as a reminder that capital is not just a tool; it's a strategic asset that, when managed wisely, becomes a bulwark against market uncertainties and a catalyst for enduring success.

CHAPTER 16

TRADING AGAINST THE TREND

In the intricate dance of financial markets, the prevailing trend is a powerful force that shapes the landscape of opportunities and risks. "Trading Against the Trend" is a perilous deviation that exposes traders to heightened risks and challenges. This chapter explores the inherent dangers associated with going against prevailing market trends, emphasizing the importance of aligning strategies with the directional currents of the market.

The Power of Market Trends

Market trends are more than mere patterns; they represent the collective sentiment and actions of market participants. Trading against the trend is akin to swimming against a powerful current, requiring significant effort and exposing traders to the risk of being swept away.

Missing the Path of Least Resistance

Trends exist because of the prevailing imbalance between buying and selling forces. Trading against the trend means missing the path of least resistance—the direction that the market is naturally inclined to move. Going against this current increases the likelihood of encountering obstacles and facing unexpected challenges.

Chasing Reversals: A Risky Endeavor

While market reversals can be lucrative, predicting them consistently is a challenging endeavor. Trading against the trend often involves attempting to catch reversals, exposing traders to the risk of mistimed entries, extended drawdowns, and missed opportunities to capitalize on the prevailing trend.

Psychological Toll of Fighting Trends

The psychological toll of trading against the trend can be significant. Constantly battling the market's prevailing direction can lead to stress, anxiety, and emotional exhaustion. Aligning with the trend, on the other hand, allows traders to ride the natural flow of the market, reducing emotional strain.

Missing Trend-Following Opportunities

Market trends provide numerous opportunities for trend-following strategies. Trading against the trend means missing out on these opportunities and the potential for sustained profits. Successful traders recognize the value of aligning with trends, leveraging momentum, and capturing the upward or downward movements in the market.

Increased Transaction Costs

Frequent trades against the trend can lead to increased transaction costs. Buying and selling against the prevailing direction often involves more frequent trades, resulting in higher commissions and slippage. This additional cost can eat into potential profits and exacerbate losses.

Risk of Significant Drawdowns

Trading against the trend exposes traders to the risk of significant drawdowns. Trends can persist longer than expected, and attempting to call the top or bottom of a market exposes traders to the potential for extended losses before a reversal occurs.

Challenging Market Timing

Market timing is a formidable challenge, especially when going against prevailing trends. Trading against the trend requires precise timing to enter and exit positions, adding an additional layer of complexity to the decision-making process.

Aligning Strategies with Market Dynamics

Successful traders recognize the importance of aligning strategies with market dynamics. Rather than fighting the prevailing trend, they seek to understand it, adapt to it, and capitalize on it. This approach involves a strategic blend of technical analysis, trend identification, and risk management.

Conclusion

"Trading Against the Trend" is a formidable challenge that tests the mettle of traders. This chapter underscores the inherent risks associated with going against prevailing market trends and emphasizes the importance of aligning strategies with the natural currents of the market. As you navigate the dynamic ebb and flow of financial markets, let this be a steadfast reminder that success often lies in recognizing, adapting to, and capitalizing on the prevailing trends that shape the ever-changing landscape of opportunities and risks.

CHAPTER 17

IGNORING MARKET SENTIMENT

In the vast and interconnected world of financial markets, the collective mood and perceptions of market participants play a crucial role in shaping price movements. "Ignoring Market Sentiment" is a pitfall that can leave traders blind to the nuanced undercurrents that influence asset prices. This chapter explores the risks associated with neglecting market sentiment and advocates for the incorporation of sentiment analysis as a valuable tool for informed decision-making.

The Unseen Force: Market Sentiment

Market sentiment is the invisible force that sways the collective mindset of traders and investors. It reflects emotions, beliefs, and expectations that can propel markets to unforeseen heights or plunge them into unexpected depths. Ignoring this dynamic force leaves traders without a key element of understanding market dynamics.

The Human Element in Trading

Financial markets are not just about numbers and charts; they are a reflection of human behavior. Ignoring market sentiment neglects the human element—the fear, greed, optimism, and pessimism that drive market participants to buy or sell. Incorporating sentiment analysis provides a more holistic view of market movements.

Identifying Trends Before They Materialize

Market sentiment often precedes observable trends. Ignoring sentiment means traders may miss the early signs of shifts in market direction. Sentiment analysis allows traders to identify emerging trends and position themselves advantageously before the broader market catches on.

Contrarian Opportunities

Contrarian trading, capitalizing on market sentiment diverging from fundamentals, is a strategy often overlooked when sentiment is ignored. Traders who incorporate sentiment analysis can identify situations where prevailing sentiment may be overly optimistic or pessimistic, presenting contrarian opportunities for profit.

Gauging Market Exuberance and Fear

Extreme market sentiment—whether exuberance or fear—can signal potential turning points. Ignoring these extremes may lead to missed opportunities or heightened risks. Sentiment analysis provides a gauge of market sentiment, helping traders navigate potential inflection points in the market.

News and Social Media Impact

In the digital age, news and social media play a significant role in shaping market sentiment. Ignoring sentiment means neglecting valuable information sources. Incorporating sentiment analysis involves monitoring news, social media chatter, and other sources to gauge the prevailing mood and sentiment.

Enhancing Risk Management

Market sentiment can impact the effectiveness of risk management strategies. Ignoring sentiment may lead to underestimating or overlooking potential risks associated with prevailing market conditions. Integrating sentiment analysis into risk management allows for a more comprehensive assessment of potential challenges.

Adapting to Changing Conditions

Markets are dynamic, and sentiment can shift rapidly. Ignoring these shifts leaves traders ill-prepared to adapt to changing conditions. Sentiment analysis enables traders to stay agile, adjusting their strategies in response to evolving market sentiment and maintaining a competitive edge.

Behavioral Finance Insights

Behavioral finance, which explores how psychological factors influence financial decision-making, is closely tied to market sentiment. Ignoring sentiment means missing out on the insights provided by this field. Traders who integrate sentiment analysis benefit from a deeper understanding of the behavioral factors driving market movements.

Conclusion

"Ignoring Market Sentiment" is a pitfall that obscures a critical aspect of trading—understanding the collective mindset that shapes market dynamics. This chapter advocates for the incorporation of sentiment analysis as an invaluable tool for informed decision-making. As you navigate the intricacies of financial markets, let this serve as a reminder that success often lies in acknowledging, interpreting, and leveraging the powerful force of market sentiment to make strategic and well-informed trading decisions.

CHAPTER 18

DEPENDENCE ON TIPS AND RUMOURS

In the vast and interconnected world of financial markets, information is currency. However, not all information is created equal, and "Dependence on Tips and Rumours" is a perilous pitfall that can lead traders astray. This chapter explores the risks associated with relying on unverified tips and market rumours and advocates for the importance of basing trading decisions on verified, well-researched information.

The Temptation of Quick Fixes

Tips and rumours often promise quick fixes and extraordinary returns. The allure of easy profits can be enticing, but dependence on such information exposes traders to the risk of making decisions without a thorough understanding of the underlying factors influencing the market.

Unreliable Sources

The financial markets are flooded with information from various sources, and not all sources are reliable. Relying on tips and rumours from unverified or questionable sources can lead to misinformation, misguided decisions, and potential financial losses.

Lack of Due Diligence

Dependence on tips and rumours often bypasses the crucial step of due diligence. Successful trading requires a comprehensive understanding of market fundamentals, trends, and potential risks. Skipping this step in favor of quick tips can leave traders ill-equipped to navigate the complexities of financial markets.

Market Manipulation

Tips and rumours can be tools for market manipulation. Unscrupulous individuals or entities may spread false information to manipulate prices for their benefit. Traders who depend on such misinformation become unwitting participants in these schemes, risking financial losses and legal repercussions.

Reputation Damage

Acting on unreliable tips and rumours can damage a trader's reputation. Consistently making decisions based on unverified information may lead to poor performance and erode trust with peers, investors, and other market participants.

Separating Noise from Signal

Financial markets are noisy, with a constant flow of information. Discerning between valuable insights and market noise is crucial. Dependence on tips and rumours often amplifies the noise, making it difficult for traders to identify genuine opportunities and risks.

Long-Term Sustainability

Successful trading is a marathon, not a sprint. Depending on tips and rumours for quick gains may yield short-term successes but is unlikely to sustain long-term profitability. Building a solid foundation based on verified information and thorough research is essential for enduring success.

The Importance of Verification

Verified information is the bedrock of informed decision-making. Traders should prioritize information from credible sources, conduct independent research, and verify the accuracy of tips before acting on them. This disciplined approach helps in making well-informed and prudent decisions.

Learning from Mistakes

Traders who depend on tips and rumours often miss the valuable lessons that come from mistakes. Acknowledging errors, analyzing their causes, and learning from them are integral parts of the trading journey. Relying on unverified information can hinder this crucial process of continuous improvement.

Conclusion

"Dependence on Tips and Rumours" is a siren call that tempts traders with promises of easy profits but often leads to treacherous waters. This chapter emphasizes the importance of basing trading decisions on verified information, thorough research, and a disciplined approach to information consumption. As you navigate the dynamic currents of financial markets, let this be a reminder that success is rooted in knowledge, diligence, and the ability to distinguish between valuable insights and market noise.

CHAPTER 19

IMPULSIVE DECISION-MAKING

In the fast-paced and unpredictable world of financial markets, impulsive decision-making is a formidable adversary that can jeopardize even the most well-thought-out strategies. This chapter explores the risks associated with impulsive decisions and advocates for the importance of cultivating discipline, patience, and a methodical approach to decision-making to avoid regrettable outcomes.

The Temptation of Instant Gratification

Impulsive decision-making often stems from the desire for instant gratification. In the quest for quick profits or the avoidance of short-term losses, traders may act without thorough analysis, exposing themselves to unforeseen risks and regrettable consequences.

Emotional Rollercoaster

Emotions play a significant role in impulsive decision-making. Fear, greed, and anxiety can lead to snap judgments that deviate from a well-defined trading plan. Managing emotions and maintaining a level-headed approach are essential to avoid being swept up in the emotional rollercoaster of impulsive decision-making.

Lack of Strategic Alignment

Impulsive decisions are often disconnected from an overarching strategy. Acting on a whim without aligning decisions with a well-thought-out plan can lead to inconsistency, making it challenging to evaluate the effectiveness of strategies and increasing the likelihood of regret.

Overlooking Risk Management

Impulsive decision-making tends to neglect risk management principles. Traders may expose themselves to excessive risks without considering potential downsides. Diligent risk assessment is crucial for protecting capital and avoiding impulsive moves that can lead to significant losses.

Failing to Learn from Past Mistakes

One hallmark of impulsive decision-making is a failure to learn from past mistakes. Traders who consistently make decisions on impulse miss valuable opportunities for reflection, improvement, and the development of a more disciplined approach to trading.

Impulsive Trading vs. Disciplined Trading

Disciplined trading involves a systematic and strategic approach, while impulsive trading is characterized by spontaneity and lack of forethought. Traders who succumb to impulsivity risk deviating from their established plans, leading to inconsistent performance and potentially regrettable outcomes.

The Illusion of Control

Impulsive decision-making often arises from an illusion of control—believing that quick actions can influence or manipulate market outcomes. Recognizing the unpredictable nature of financial markets is essential to avoid falling into the trap of making impulsive decisions based on this illusion.

Cultivating Patience

Patience is the antidote to impulsivity. Cultivating patience involves waiting for optimal trading setups, thoroughly analyzing market conditions, and making decisions based on a well-defined strategy. Patience allows traders to resist the urge for instant gratification and make decisions with a long-term perspective.

Incorporating Deliberation into Decision-Making

Deliberation is the cornerstone of sound decision-making. Taking the time to analyze market trends, assess risk-reward ratios, and align actions with a predefined strategy minimizes the likelihood of impulsive decisions. Deliberate decision-making enhances consistency and helps traders avoid unnecessary pitfalls.

Conclusion

"Impulsive Decision-Making" is a treacherous path that can lead traders astray in the dynamic landscape of financial markets. This chapter underscores the risks associated with impulsive actions and emphasizes the importance of cultivating discipline, patience, and a deliberate approach to decision-making. As you navigate the complexities and uncertainties of financial markets, let this be a steadfast reminder that success is not found in the impulsivity of the moment but in the disciplined and thoughtful decisions that stand the test of time.

CHAPTER 20

DISREGARDING GLOBAL EVENTS

In the interconnected and globalized landscape of financial markets, overlooking the influence of global events is a perilous oversight. This chapter explores the risks associated with disregarding the impact of global events and emphasizes the importance of staying informed about geopolitical, economic, and social developments to make well-informed trading decisions.

The Global Ripple Effect

Global events send ripples through financial markets, transcending borders and impacting various asset classes. Disregarding these events is akin to navigating turbulent waters without a compass, leaving traders exposed to unexpected market movements and volatility.

Geopolitical Uncertainties

Geopolitical events, such as geopolitical conflicts, elections, and diplomatic tensions, can significantly affect market sentiment and asset prices. Disregarding these events leaves traders vulnerable to sudden shifts in investor perceptions and sentiment, potentially resulting in unexpected market reactions.

Economic Indicators and Data Releases

Economic indicators and data releases from major economies are vital factors influencing financial markets. Disregarding key economic events, such as employment reports, GDP figures, and central bank announcements, hampers a trader's ability to anticipate market movements and adjust strategies accordingly.

Currency Fluctuations

Global events have a profound impact on currency markets. Disregarding shifts in geopolitical alliances, economic policies, or trade agreements can lead to miscalculations in currency trends, affecting the performance of portfolios with international exposure.

Commodity Price Volatility

Commodities, such as oil, gold, and agricultural products, are sensitive to global events. Disregarding geopolitical tensions, weather-related phenomena, or supply chain disruptions can result in unanticipated commodity price fluctuations, affecting industries and sectors globally.

Social and Environmental Factors

Social and environmental events, including protests, natural disasters, and climate-related developments, can influence investor sentiment and market dynamics. Disregarding these factors may leave traders exposed to unforeseen risks that impact asset valuations.

Interconnected Financial Markets

Global financial markets are interconnected, and events in one part of the world can reverberate across continents. Disregarding these interconnections can lead to a narrow perspective on market movements, hindering the ability to anticipate broader trends and correlations.

Technological Advancements

Technological advancements and innovations are global drivers of change. Disregarding developments in technology, such as blockchain, artificial intelligence, or cybersecurity threats, may result in missed opportunities or increased vulnerability to emerging risks.

Shifts in Monetary Policy

Central banks worldwide play a pivotal role in shaping monetary policies. Disregarding shifts in interest rates, quantitative easing measures, or changes in central bank rhetoric can lead to misinterpretations of market directions and missed opportunities.

Risk Management and Contingency Planning

Disregarding global events jeopardizes effective risk management and contingency planning. Traders who overlook the potential impact of unforeseen global developments may find themselves ill-prepared to navigate market uncertainties and mitigate potential losses.

Staying Informed and Adapting Strategies

To navigate the complexities of global financial markets successfully, traders must stay informed about geopolitical, economic, and social events. Adapting strategies based on a comprehensive understanding of global dynamics enhances the ability to make well-informed decisions and capitalize on opportunities.

Conclusion

"Disregarding Global Events" is a pitfall that undermines the foundation of informed decision-making in the dynamic world of financial markets. This chapter emphasizes the critical importance of acknowledging and understanding the impact of global events on market dynamics. As you navigate the ever-changing landscape of financial markets, let this be a steadfast reminder that success lies not just in analyzing charts and indicators but in embracing a global perspective that encompasses the myriad factors shaping the intricate tapestry of global finance.

CHAPTER 21

UNCHECKED LEVERAGE

Leverage is a double-edged sword in the world of trading, capable of amplifying both gains and losses. "Unchecked Leverage" is a perilous pitfall that can lead traders down a treacherous path, exposing them to significant risks and the potential for devastating losses. This chapter explores the dangers of excessive leverage and emphasizes the importance of prudent risk management to safeguard trading capital.

The Allure of Magnified Profits

Leverage allows traders to control a larger position size with a relatively smaller amount of capital. While this can amplify profits, the allure of magnified gains often tempts traders to use excessive leverage without fully considering the corresponding increase in risk.

Magnifying Losses Exponentially

Unchecked leverage has the potential to magnify losses exponentially. Even a small adverse market movement can lead to significant account drawdowns when high levels of leverage are employed. Traders who overlook this risk may find themselves in a precarious financial situation.

Margin Calls and Forced Liquidations

Excessive leverage increases the likelihood of margin calls, where traders are required to deposit additional funds to cover potential losses. Failure to meet margin requirements can result in forced liquidations, selling positions at unfavorable prices and compounding losses.

Psychological Impact

The psychological impact of unchecked leverage is profound. Large, sudden losses can induce panic, fear, and emotional distress, leading to impaired decision-making. The stress associated with significant losses may cloud judgment and hinder a trader's ability to recover effectively.

Underestimating Market Volatility

Market conditions can change rapidly, and unchecked leverage leaves traders vulnerable to unexpected volatility. Failure to account for potential market fluctuations can result in positions being liquidated during adverse conditions, compounding losses.

Capital Erosion and Account Blowouts

Unchecked leverage poses a significant risk to capital preservation. Traders who expose themselves to excessive leverage may experience rapid capital erosion and, in extreme cases, account blowouts, leading to a loss of trading capital and hindering future trading endeavors.

Long-Term Viability

The long-term viability of a trading career is jeopardized by unchecked leverage. Sustainable success in trading requires a focus on capital preservation and consistent, disciplined risk management. Traders who prioritize unchecked leverage over prudent risk practices may struggle to endure in the competitive world of trading.

The Importance of Risk Management

Risk management is the antidote to the perils of unchecked leverage. Establishing well-defined risk parameters, using stop-loss orders, and sizing positions based on a careful consideration of potential losses are essential elements of effective risk management.

Balancing Risk and Reward

Successful traders understand the delicate balance between risk and reward. While leverage can enhance returns, it must be used judiciously to avoid disproportionate exposure to potential losses. Striking the right balance allows traders to capitalize on opportunities while managing risks responsibly.

Regularly Assessing Risk Tolerance

Risk tolerance is dynamic and can change based on market conditions, personal circumstances, and trading experiences. Traders must regularly reassess their risk tolerance and adjust their use of leverage accordingly to ensure alignment with their overall risk management strategy.

Conclusion

"Unchecked Leverage" is a formidable adversary that can undermine the foundations of successful trading. This chapter underscores the dangers of excessive leverage and highlights the importance of prudent risk management as an essential safeguard against potential pitfalls. As you navigate the intricate landscape of financial markets, let this serve as a steadfast reminder that success in trading is not solely about maximizing gains but also about protecting your capital with diligence and discipline.

CHAPTER 22

TRADING WITHOUT A SAFETY NET

In the unpredictable terrain of financial markets, the absence of a safety net can transform routine challenges into potentially insurmountable obstacles. "Trading without a Safety Net" is a perilous oversight that leaves traders vulnerable to unexpected setbacks. This chapter delves into the significance of having an emergency fund to navigate uncertainties, mitigate risks, and fortify resilience in the dynamic world of trading.

The Unpredictability of Financial Markets

Financial markets are inherently unpredictable, subject to sudden shifts, unforeseen events, and volatile conditions. Trading without a safety net exposes traders to the full force of these uncertainties, leaving little room to absorb unexpected blows to capital.

Mitigating Unforeseen Losses

An emergency fund serves as a buffer against unforeseen losses. Whether triggered by market downturns, unexpected expenses, or personal challenges, having a safety net allows traders to weather temporary setbacks without jeopardizing their overall trading capital.

Protection against Margin Calls

Margin calls can be a sudden and unavoidable reality in leveraged trading. Without a safety net, traders may struggle to meet margin requirements, leading to forced liquidations and potential losses. An emergency fund acts as a protective barrier, reducing the risk of margin-related complications.

Managing Personal and Financial Emergencies

Life is replete with unexpected twists, both personal and financial. A safety net provides a financial cushion to manage emergencies such as health issues, family crises, or unforeseen expenses. Trading without this safety net amplifies the impact of external challenges on a trader's financial stability.

Psychological Resilience

Knowing that there is a safety net in place fosters psychological resilience. The confidence that comes from having a financial cushion enables traders to approach decision-making with a clear mind, reducing the emotional stress associated with trading uncertainties.

Flexibility in Decision-Making

An emergency fund provides flexibility in decision-making. Traders with a safety net can take a more measured approach to opportunities and risks, avoiding the pressure to make impulsive decisions due to financial constraints.

Building Confidence in Risk-Taking

Confidence is a vital component of successful trading. A safety net empowers traders to take calculated risks and explore new strategies without the paralyzing fear of catastrophic losses. This confidence is conducive to growth and adaptability in the ever-evolving landscape of financial markets.

Determining the Size of the Safety Net

The size of an emergency fund depends on individual circumstances, trading style, and risk tolerance. Traders should assess their monthly living expenses, potential trading losses, and other financial obligations to determine an appropriate size for their safety net.

Balancing Capital Allocation

Maintaining a safety net involves a delicate balance between allocating capital for trading and preserving funds for emergencies. Striking this balance requires a thoughtful approach to risk management and financial planning.

Continuous Monitoring and Adjustment

An emergency fund is not a static entity; it requires continuous monitoring and adjustment. Traders should regularly reassess their financial situation, update their safety net based on changing circumstances, and ensure that it remains aligned with their evolving needs.

Conclusion

"Trading without a Safety Net" is a high-wire act that exposes traders to unnecessary risks and challenges. This chapter underscores the importance of having an emergency fund as a safeguard against unforeseen setbacks. As you navigate the dynamic landscape of financial markets, let this be a steadfast reminder that success in trading is not just about maximizing gains but also about fortifying your resilience and ensuring the stability of your financial foundation.

CHAPTER 23

NEGLECTING PERSONAL WELL-BEING

In the relentless pursuit of trading success, it's easy for traders to overlook a crucial aspect—their own well-being. "Neglecting Personal Well-being" is a perilous oversight that can compromise physical health, mental resilience, and overall life satisfaction. This chapter explores the importance of striking a balance between trading ambitions and personal well-being for sustained success in both arenas.

The Toll of Constant Screen Time

Trading often involves prolonged periods of screen time, exposing traders to the risks of eye strain, headaches, and fatigue. Neglecting breaks and physical movement can lead to a sedentary lifestyle, impacting overall health and well-being.

Stress and its Impact on Decision-Making

The high-stakes nature of trading can induce significant stress. Neglecting stress management not only affects mental health but can impair cognitive functions, leading to suboptimal decision-making. Prioritizing personal well-being is essential for maintaining a clear and focused mind during trading activities.

Sleep Deprivation and Trading Performance

In the 24/7 world of global markets, traders may find themselves sacrificing sleep for market monitoring. Neglecting adequate sleep disrupts cognitive function, emotional resilience, and overall trading performance. Recognizing the importance of quality sleep is integral to long-term success.

Isolation and the Importance of Social Connection

Trading can be a solitary endeavor, leading to feelings of isolation. Neglecting social connections can impact mental health and hinder emotional well-being. Cultivating a support network and maintaining social ties are crucial for a balanced and fulfilling life.

Physical Fitness for Long-Term Resilience

Sedentary trading habits can contribute to a decline in physical fitness. Neglecting regular exercise not only impacts health but also diminishes the resilience needed to navigate the challenges of trading. Incorporating physical activity into daily routines is an investment in long-term well-being.

Dietary Habits and Cognitive Function

Nutrition plays a vital role in cognitive function and overall well-being. Neglecting healthy dietary habits can lead to fatigue, mood swings, and diminished mental clarity. Prioritizing nutritious food choices supports sustained energy levels and optimal cognitive performance.

Burnout and the Importance of Balance

The relentless pursuit of trading success can lead to burnout. Neglecting work-life balance contributes to emotional exhaustion, reduced productivity, and a diminished passion for trading. Striking a balance between professional ambitions and personal life is essential for sustained enthusiasm and resilience.

Recognizing Signs of Mental Health Struggles

Trading challenges can take a toll on mental health. Neglecting signs of stress, anxiety, or depression can exacerbate these issues. Acknowledging and addressing mental health struggles is a proactive step toward maintaining overall well-being.

Incorporating Mindfulness and Relaxation

Mindfulness and relaxation techniques are valuable tools for managing stress. Neglecting these practices deprives traders of effective strategies for staying grounded and focused. Integrating mindfulness into daily routines fosters a calm and composed mindset.

Regular Health Check-ups

Neglecting regular health check-ups is a common oversight in the pursuit of trading success. Prioritizing preventive healthcare allows traders to address potential issues early, ensuring physical well-being and providing peace of mind.

Conclusion

"Neglecting Personal Well-being" is a pitfall that undermines the foundation of sustained success in trading. This chapter emphasizes the importance of balancing trading ambitions with physical and mental well-being. As you navigate the demands of financial markets, let this be a steadfast reminder that personal health is not a trade-off for success but an integral component that contributes to resilience, clarity of mind, and overall life satisfaction.

CHAPTER 24

BLINDLY TRUSTING EXPERTS

In the vast and complex world of financial markets, the allure of expert opinions is ever-present. However, "Blindly Trusting Experts" is a perilous pitfall that can undermine a trader's ability to navigate the dynamic landscape of investments. This chapter explores the importance of critical thinking and independent analysis in the face of expert advice and emphasizes the need for traders to cultivate their own insights for long-term success.

The Appeal of Expert Opinions

Expert opinions, whether from financial analysts, market commentators, or renowned investors, carry weight in the trading community. The allure of tapping into the knowledge of those deemed experts is understandable, but blind reliance on their views can lead to pitfalls.

The Limitations of Expertise

Even seasoned experts can be fallible. Markets are influenced by a multitude of factors, and no single expert possesses a crystal ball. Blindly trusting experts neglects the inherent limitations of forecasting and the uncertainties that define financial markets.

Conflicting Expert Views

The financial landscape often witnesses conflicting expert opinions. One expert may be bullish on a particular asset, while another is bearish. Blind trust in experts without critical evaluation can leave traders confused and exposed to potential market misjudgments.

Hidden Agendas and Conflicts of Interest

Experts, like anyone else, may have hidden agendas or conflicts of interest. Blindly following their advice without considering potential biases can lead traders down a path that serves the interests of the expert rather than the trader's own financial goals.

Evolving Market Conditions

Markets are dynamic, and conditions change. What worked in the past for an expert may not be applicable to current market dynamics. Blindly adhering to outdated advice can hinder a trader's ability to adapt to evolving market conditions.

The Importance of Independent Analysis

Independent analysis is the bedrock of sound decision-making. Traders should critically evaluate expert opinions, considering their own risk tolerance, financial goals, and market insights.

Independent analysis empowers traders to make decisions aligned with their unique circumstances.

Developing a Personal Trading Style

Blindly following expert advice can hinder the development of a personal trading style. Each trader has a unique risk appetite, preferred timeframes, and financial objectives. Cultivating independence allows traders to tailor strategies that align with their individual preferences and goals.

Continuous Learning and Adaptation

Financial markets are ever-changing, and successful traders recognize the need for continuous learning. Blindly trusting experts without engaging in ongoing education and self-improvement hampers a trader's ability to adapt to new market trends and strategies.

Utilizing Expert Advice as a Tool

Rather than blindly trusting experts, traders should view their advice as one of many tools in their analytical toolbox. Experts can provide valuable insights, but these should be considered alongside independent research, technical analysis, and a thorough understanding of market fundamentals.

Risk Management and Decision Accountability

Traders who blindly follow expert advice may struggle with accountability for their decisions. Effective risk management involves taking responsibility for one's choices. Blind trust in experts can diminish a trader's sense of ownership and accountability in their trading journey.

Conclusion

"Blindly Trusting Experts" is a pitfall that can undermine a trader's ability to navigate the intricate world of financial markets. This chapter underscores the importance of critical thinking, independent analysis, and a discerning approach to expert opinions. As you chart your course through the dynamic landscape of trading, let this be a reminder that success is not found in blindly following the crowd but in the thoughtful and independent decisions that align with your unique trading objectives.

CHAPTER 25

STAYING RESILIENT

In the unpredictable realm of financial markets, resilience is a trait that separates enduring traders from those who succumb to challenges. "Staying Resilient" is not just a desirable quality; it's a crucial skill that empowers traders to navigate the inevitable ups and downs of trading with fortitude and adaptability. This chapter delves into the importance of developing resilience and offers insights into cultivating this essential quality for long-term success.

Acknowledging the Inherent Uncertainties

Financial markets are inherently uncertain, marked by volatility, unpredictability, and unforeseen events. Resilient traders acknowledge these inherent uncertainties and understand that losses and setbacks are an integral part of the trading journey.

Embracing a Growth Mindset

A growth mindset is foundational to resilience. Traders with a growth mindset view challenges as opportunities for learning and improvement. Rather than seeing setbacks as failures, they see them as stepping stones toward mastery and success.

Learning from Mistakes

Resilience involves learning from mistakes. Traders who can analyze their errors, understand the root causes, and implement corrective measures are better equipped to bounce back from setbacks. Each mistake becomes a valuable lesson in the journey toward mastery.

Fostering Emotional Intelligence

Emotional intelligence is a key component of resilience. Traders who can recognize and manage their emotions effectively are better positioned to navigate the emotional rollercoaster of trading. Emotional resilience enables sound decision-making even in the face of adversity.

Maintaining a Long-Term Perspective

Resilient traders maintain a long-term perspective. They understand that short-term fluctuations and losses are part of the broader journey. This perspective helps in weathering temporary setbacks without losing sight of the overarching trading goals.

Adapting to Changing Market Conditions

Markets evolve, and resilient traders adapt. They embrace change, stay informed about evolving market conditions, and adjust their strategies accordingly. Adaptability is a hallmark of resilience in the face of dynamic market landscapes.

Building a Support Network

Resilience is reinforced by a robust support network. Traders who can rely on mentors, peers, and a community of like-minded individuals find strength in shared experiences. A supportive network provides encouragement during challenging times and celebrates successes together.

Balancing Confidence and Humility

Resilient traders strike a balance between confidence and humility. While confidence is crucial for making decisive moves, humility allows for introspection, continuous learning, and an openness to new insights. This balance enhances resilience in the face of both successes and failures.

Setting Realistic Expectations

Resilience is nurtured by setting realistic expectations. Traders who understand that trading is a journey with ups and downs, rather than a linear path to constant success, are better prepared to handle the inevitable challenges that arise.

Cultivating Patience

Patience is a cornerstone of resilience. Markets may not always move in the desired direction immediately, and setbacks may require time to overcome. Cultivating patience allows traders to stay focused on long-term objectives and endure the natural ebb and flow of trading.

Celebrating Small Wins

Resilience is fueled by acknowledging and celebrating small wins. Each success, regardless of size, contributes to a trader's confidence and reinforces the belief that progress is being made. Celebrating victories, no matter how minor, builds positive momentum.

Conclusion

"Staying Resilient" is not just a trait; it's a dynamic skill that evolves through experience, self-awareness, and a commitment to continuous growth. This chapter underscores the importance of resilience in navigating the challenges of trading. As you navigate the dynamic landscape of financial markets, let this be a reminder that success is not defined solely by profits but also by the ability to persevere, adapt, and thrive in the face of adversity.

May your trading journey be marked by the resilience to withstand challenges, the wisdom to learn from setbacks, and the unwavering determination to achieve enduring success in the ever-evolving world of financial markets.